Book Ends for the Reader

Topic: Summer and Health

Notes to Parents and Teachers:

The books your child reads at this level will have more of a storyline with details to discuss. Have children practice reading more fluently at this level. Take turns reading pages with your child so you can model what fluent reading sounds like.

REMEMBER: PRAISE IS A GREAT MOTIVATOR!
Here are some praise points for beginning readers:

• I love how you read that sentence so it sounded just like you were talking.

• Great job reading that sentence like a question!

• WOW! You read that page with such good expression!

Let's Make Paired Reading Connections:

• First, read the fiction text, ***Not Yet!*** by Robert Rosen.

• Next, read the nonfiction text, ***Who Makes Rules?***

• Discuss how the pictures in the books look different. *One has drawings. One has photographs.*

Not Yet!

• What are both books about? _____. What a book is about is called a topic.

• Who is making the rules at the pool in the story ***Not Yet?***

• Who is making the rules at the pool in this book?

Table of Contents

Rourke
Educational Media
rourkeeducationalmedia.com

Can you find these words?

bus

lifeguard

rules

safe

Who Makes Rules?

Rules tell us how to act.

rules

PLAYGROUND RULES:

1. PLAY AT YOUR OWN RISK.
2. NO PROFANITY.
3. NO CLIMBING UP SLI
5. NO ROUGH

3

Who makes rules at school?

4

Teachers make the rules.

Who makes rules at home?

Parents make the rules.

Who makes rules on the **bus**?

bus

Bus drivers make the rules.

lifeguard

Who makes rules at the pool?

A **lifeguard** makes the rules.

Rules help us get along.

Rules keep us **safe.**

Did you find these words?

Who makes rules on the **bus**?

A **lifeguard** makes the rules.

Rules tell us how to act.

Rules keep us **safe**.

Photo Glossary

 **bus** (buhs): A large vehicle that carries many people.

 **lifeguard** (life-gahrd): An expert swimmer who is trained to rescue swimmers when they are in danger.

 **rules** (roolz): Instructions that tell us what to do and help keep us safe.

 **safe** (sayf): Protected from danger.

Index

About the Author

Savina Collins lives in Florida with her husband and five adventurous kids. Savina enjoys watching her kids surf and the pelicans dive for fish!

www.rourkeeducationalmedia.com

PHOTO CREDITS: Cover: ©muharrem öner; p.2,8-9,14,15: ©martinedoucet; p.2,10-11,14,15: ©Gene Chutka; p.2,3,14,15: ©Spcteam | Dreamstime.com; p.2,13,14,15: © kajakik; p.4-5: ©kristian sekulic; p.6-7: ©monkeybusinessimages; p.12: ©FatCamera

Edited by: Keli Sipperley
Cover and interior design by: Rhea Magaro-Wallace

Library of Congress PCN Data
Who Makes Rules? / Savina Collins
(I Know)
ISBN (hard cover)(alk. paper) 978-1-64156-174-7
ISBN (soft cover) 978-1-64156-230-0
ISBN (e-Book) 978-1-64156-283-6
Library of Congress Control Number: 2017957784

Printed in the United States of America, North Mankato, Minnesota

Book Ends for the Reader

I know...

1. Who makes the rules at school?

2. Who makes the rules on the bus?

3. Where does the lifeguard make the rules?

I think ...

1. Why do you think we need rules?

2. What is a rule you have at school?

3. Did you ever make a rule?